CHILD SEXUAL
ABUSE

BEULAH COATS

Child Sexual Abuse : It's Alright to Tell
Copyright © 2023 Beulah Coats

Library of Congress Control Number: 2023911839
Paperback: 979-8-9886071-2-0

CONTENTS

CONTENTS

CHILD SEXUAL ABUSE

Child sexual abuse is at an all time high millions of children will be victims of molestation. One Out of every girl and boy will be sexually assaulted at some point in their lives something has to Be done. Why is society pushing it aside as if it can wait and not that important? There has to be National and community attention before we have any hope of stomping out sexual abuse and Abuse of any kind. Just think of all the silent cries of so many children that can't be heard can You even imagine what they have to endure, Justice what justice for who? The predator our the Victims in and out of court that's what happens in our court rooms. When will there be better Laws enforced It's hard to believe that a child can be raped are molested and some times worse And in most cases there predators are set free.

Something is wrong not just someone the painful truth is most of the time it comes from inside the family, Parents, Grandparents, stepparents, cousins, uncles, incest sexual contact Between relatives. If you are someone you know are being abuse please report it IT'S ALRIGHT TO TELL. By writing this book it has helped me release a lot of anger, pain And guilt that I've had inside for too long. Raped by my father's friend at a very early age not Knowing what was happening but new it was something wrong. Touched and fondled by one of my grandfathers that one is still heard to deal with. Telling me I was a pretty little girl and come Back to see him how disgusting and sick is that. Our children need to be talked to about sex it's All around so it's easy to talk about tell your children if someone touches them tell someone And don't be afraid. If anyone makes any advances toward them that they can come to you and Tell. Raped by my mothers boy friend what could I do seeing him with my mother then having Him all over me. No one told me that I could tell so I kept it inside trying not let it be known What was happening to me. The biggest problem is telling the shame and guilt you feel and Not knowing what to do are who to turn to and how they will feel about you.Sex isn't wrong Sexual abuse is someone has to stand up and fight for the children IT'S NOT A CHOICE IT'S A CHILD. So many of our children are being abused and their innocence taken away at such an Early age 3 and 4 years old. Imagine the pain and wondering what is going on I know the pain Of abuse raped twice and had to stay my distance from my own kin. When I was older I know it Was wrong but to embarrassed and afraid to tell. Thinking it was my fault and not knowing any better so I put it inside of me never to let it come out. When I was raped by my fathers' friend This was his friend what could I say why was I around him was it my fault I couldn't let them know I didn't understand it myself. My mothers boy friend what could I tell her I felt so guilty and it wasn't my fault but I felt like it I didn't want to hurt her. But by not telling is worse if you let it go and not talk it gets harder to tell and the guilt will take over your mind. I still carry this with me and it hurts knowing I should of told her. Our children shouldn't be afraid to tell their parents about whatever is happening to them she had the right to know what he was doing to me. Sex should be like any other subject sexual abuse is a crime and should be treated as such it will not go away and will affect your life in some kind of way. My mother's boy friend was so nice and kind to me there wasn't anything he wouldn't do for me. He would buy my cloths and shoes for school and anything I needed to get my mothers trust and mind.Hetook the attention off me by helping my brothers and then ask me to go with him like any other time I went. But this time he took me off along and told me what he was going to do.I tried to fight him off but he was so much bigger than me it was hard he was raping me but I was still fighting and trying to push him off.I couldn't believe what he was doing to me not this man that I trusted and my Mother's boy friend. He said if I told she wouldn't believe me so how could I bring myself to tell her something like this would she believe me are him. So I put it deep inside never to bring it out my mother how could I tell her something like this. But just how much can you put inside Without it eating at your soul, body and mind as a young girl I have been raped and molested trying to stay away from family and friends .What do you do I felt so dirty and ashamed it was like I let this happen to me and by not telling is when the guilt comes in.

So if a wound is left untreated it gets worse and harder to heal you just can't talk about it. I Think a lot about how I should of trusted my mother and told. How do you cope with something like this? The first step is talking to someone that's the key to unlocking the doors that can help. It's alright to tell the disgusting and degrading crimes against a Childs body how sick is that? Who is protecting the children? Better laws enforced to many of our children are being Violated. There are so many sick minded people out there taking over our children's body and Controlling their minds. The punishment definitely don't fit the crime it could be family, friends School and even their church no one is above suspicion. It could happen to your child at any Given time our children need protection no matter what the cost.

Wrong Turns And Feelings Sometimes without the right help and counseling that is needed we sometimes make the Wrong turns Drugs, Alcohol, Depression, and even sex.Sometimes sexual abuse can lead to sex You feel that you are no longer clean and worthy of anything are anyone. Most young girls will Be in a relationship of abuse and prostitution this kind of reaction is unreal but true. The pain Will go away but the scares never do sad, angry, and confused something has to be done and Now our babies can't wait any longer.Chil abuse isn't always easy to detect we must no matter How little find out what is happening to are children and by who. How can they hope for are Children to heal when they can walk down the street and pass their offender justice where how Can this be justiftyed? As a child of abuse I should know the signs of abuse and recognize it but By denying it and putting it in the back of my mind you can't see. I had to young girls come to To me and always ask to go home with me continually every time they would see me why couldn't I see the Pain. I looked over the obvious both of these girls were being abuse by stepparents .I know both of them that's why I couldn't see what was happening but with me being raped I should of saw the signs are at least looked into it.I should of have realized something was wrong my own child telling me she didn't like going with this person and still Iooked over it. Just because I know him the signs are always there we just have to take the time to see them and listen to what they are trying to tell us.

Special attention was given to one of these girls but just by knowing the person you wouldn't think anything like this could happen. She finally came to me and told what was happening to her it was hard but she wanted it to stop and just couldn't take anymore. She new I would do something about it this child didn't know what to do but she trusted me it was the shame that took her so long. That's why it's so important to teach are children that if they are violated it's all right to tell and come to you. This was my baby and it tore my heart apart A TIME TO KILL was good at that time. When a child has been abused it takes away more than their innocence their self-esteem and respect for them selves how do you get that back. Just take a walk in my shoes and tell me how you feel when the offender walks the streets with no regard to what he has done. When he was set free my heart almost drooped from my body why her offender set free was. When her mind and body are still lost and confused when I walk in her room at night and see the barricades she has put in front of her door where's the justice in that. When I walk beside her bed she jumps and thinks it's her offender. When she cries to me and I see all the pain inside and can't do anything about it show me the justice in that. When she shakes in her bed I can see myself in her being raped and molested even by one of my own grandfathers. How he would put his hands on me what a disgusting and confusing state that put me in. Had to put that inside and just forget that's when a child goes inside themselves and hide so no will know. Abuse is a sickness if left untreated it will spread over the body like a pledge writing this book is helping me break through the pain but with all the abuse I see it's very hard. Don't let this happen in your childs life talk and tell your child about sex, and sexual abuse don't make the mistake of being ashamed it could cast your child. We have to look into anything no matter how little it seems look at the girls who begged for help and I just didn't see the pain. I never would have thought they were being abused get in somebody's business sex abuse is everybodys business and help stop a child from hurting. Maybe if I had of took the time to listen more I could of stop the pain they were in and made a difference. No one can ask the question if you are being abused why you don't tell someone if you haven't been there you don't know the pain and embarrassment it leaves behind. After I had been raped I always felt that

I had to be on my guard at all times and wanted the love and approval of my family. There's a need to feel protected and you do whatever to get it there are so many that turn the wrong way. Know some that have turned to sex for a need to feel wanted some fear intimate relationships and others crave them. Sometimes drugs become your relief and just want to stay high and never come down to the pain anymore. Seek help express your feelings with someone the longer you wait and keep it inside the more it hurts. The sadness and loneliness will continue please tell your child you are there for them and will love and support them in any way you can. There are so many ways a child can be abused and used watch out for them the predators are always there. The question is asked again who is protecting the children are they at the hands of anyone's prey? When does it stop how many more of our babies have to be victims before laws are changed for our childrens sake. Our children are feeling more lost and afraid every day from abuse but we can't spank are child and correct them without fear of being arrested. The children are hurting teach them what is wrong and right about sex and they can come to you anytime. Reports show that a child offender will molest again after they have been released on probation that's why monitoring is very important. The safety and well-being of our children is a stake it's heart breaking just to think of it no child should have to face this alone. Teach little children about their body parts and if anyone touches them to come and let you know make sure your child feels comfortable about talking to you. Our children are crying and can't be heard wanting and needing someone to intervene and make it right and stop the pain.

Child photography the nude pictures and videos of children for the intent to entertain why is this kind of trash permitted. You can excess anything about a child why is sociality so excepting of this and willing to turn the other way. There are even priest hiding behind the church to molest our young boys and girls.Dening the problem only makes it worse and the destruction of our children will continue even in the hands of their family, church and school. Despite all the numbers and reports child abuse is still raising it's a tragedy that our children are not safe anywhere.

OPEN COMMUNICATION

Spend as much time with your child as possible and be open minded about everything and it could make a good impact on how our children feel. There are so many cases of abuse please take the time to Listen and observe your child it will make a difference .If anyone takes special interest in your child are spends a great deal of time don't hesitate to ask questions. Talk to your child about sex and maybe will talk to you about sexual abuse let them know you are there.Sex isn't the issue here sexual abuse is watch over our little children and make sure nothing is wrong ask them if someone has hurt them. We need more media courage sex is all round and should be more easy to talk about TV, movies and everywhere we turn it's about sex.Mothers against child sexual abuse marching on Washington whatever it takes march on and free our children. The unthinkable could happen at any given time if our law makers and legislature hard the cry of their own would it make a difference? A time to kill can you understand it better now. But yet we can't take the law into our own hands it's there to protect us but who is protecting the children when their predators Rome free. I have learn so much about abuse been around it a lot now I know that I should have told my mother she would have understood and done the right thing. Communication is very important it takes trust for a child to come to you. I am a survivor of sexual abuse but with all the injustice how can I move on without thinking of all the children who are still hurting and crying from abuse. The media could make a big difference in a Victims ability to heal more courage on the predator and what is happening with them. If they were convicted and monitored not just put back on the streets without any remorse. There's a lot more men coming fourth reporting of their abuse seeking justice and struggling to find who they are. Sometimes keeping it all inside can hurt more than telling someone that you can trust and talk to and release the pain. There are so many difference signs of abuse watch out for sadness, Anger, withdraws from family and friends. Displays any difference in their behavior there's a need for concern small children may complain of hurting, crying,fear of the dark, and people. Sexual abuse always has so kind of rewards such as special attention, gifts, any way of getting their trust. Other ways of taking control telling them all families do this and not to tell. Pedophiles adults who desires are directed toward children take advantage of the trust that the child has in them very rarely are they strangers. Visit your Childs day care make surprise visits at school and at home baby sitters. Be aware of any changes in your child behavior always give your attention and listen. There are all kinds of abuse we need all parents fighting in the prevention of all abuse. Mothers and fathers in the war against their children find a way to get involved and help, without hope and dreams what future do our children have That's way I hope this book is read to give hope and help anyone who is being abused come fourth and tell someone. They say together we can a difference but first we must come together as a nation and stop all abuse sexual, verbal, emotional, and neglect. There are more people worrying about who the biggest star is are who won the game last night than how many babies were molested last night. How many went to bed Hungary and how many are still crying from hurting from being abused. We have the groups, organization but better communication to prevent abuse before it happens that's what we need. How many sex offenders are set free every day is there no justice then how can we fight abuse? The media is focusing more on what's happening in Hollywood than profiling the predators of our children. How many signs did you see about how many babies were molested last night? Do you know the ones that were beaten? How many had to cry themselves to sleep from being abused. How many did you say you saw if you could just see the pain maybe it make a difference. I have been abused lived with an abused child talked to abuse children how can a Country turn its back. Billions spent on men in space children crying and trembling in their beds at night justice. Abused and left with little are no hope pushed aside as if they can wait our children are crying waiting enough. Legisture and government have to stand up and say stop and do something about it. And we as parents must join the fight and take our responsibility to protect and report any kind of abuse no matter who it is. We can form groups educate and have are child abuse organizations and agencies but until we have stricter laws against child abuse the fight is useless.

Abuse destroys self-esteem justice where are you for whom the victim are the predator? Less than 3 percent of sex offenders are prosecuted justice when you can't sleep at night, when your body hurts drugs, alcohol, and prostitution. Has attempted suicide, emotional problems how much more affliction must our children suffer before they have justice? Predators of children it's a sickness and to be treaded not put on probation. A predator spends ten years in prison then released does this mean they want molest again wrong. There are some states that are tough on second time offenders, but if they were treated the first time maybe there wouldn't be a second time. If you have a sick mind directed toward the abuse are molestation of a child a few years in a jail cell will not cure it. When you Liston to a child talk and cry about what has happen to them then you come to me and talk about justice. When their predators walk the streets yes they are labeled as molesters but does this soften the impact of the pain. How many billboards do you see each day about an abused child? How many magazines do you open and read about it? What's the cover up We need a task force on abuse more advertising, announcements, the support of the whole community participating. Appealing to the government and ligature to support the struggle to stop abuse there's got to be a better way. The numbers are so staggering that it's unbelievable prosecutors need to prosecute to have justice served we need justice.

Everybody should demand immediate attention to the countless acts of abuse that are justice system seems to not realize the impact of this crime. Better foundations of establishing the best means possible of dealing with offenders. We need not stop searching for answers with all the emotional scars left on victims of abuse. The discussion should be obvious world wide effort to promote awareness of this problem. According to a study a child is abused every second we must work to reverse their numbers Appeals, protects, to further the cause to stop abuse. Pictures on billboards, mortaring, and congress should have funding and resources available when needed to knock down all barriers of abuse. The system is faulted for so many offenders on the streets instead of treatment centers the numbers will triple if something more isn't done soon. Our children are endangered spices of their own kind fighting to be free from the hands of abuse.

THE STRUGGLE

What course can we take demonstrate, demand, that officials take a difference look at child predators. Stop denying the importance of confronting the nations growing problem of child molesters most of the punishment is unacceptable. When babies are still crying and hurting nationwide a bill that would stop pardoning offenders and put them in treatment. Boundaries need to be set victims have to deal with emotional problems and scares for the rest of their lives regardless of the outcome. When their bodies have been violated and the embarrassment of what has happen feeling like you just can't deal anymore who will take the blame. While the officials are looking the other way refusing to acknowledge the seriousness of the impact this has on a child. We can change the statistics by standing and fighting back it's an epidemic that will keep on spreading. Let's give the victims a change to heal and conquer this violation of their bodies and move on News Media, Massages, and influencing telling victims that it's alright to tell. When every i hear of a child that's been abused it brings back all the guilt, anger, at myself that I still have inside. The responsible lies on are protectors to impose sticker penalties and taking any means possible to insure immediate action. The things I have been told the cries I hear some thinking about killing themselves others wondering why it's happen to them and who to blame and not to blame. Knowing that nothing will ever be the same anymore that their whole life has changed but no matter how we look at it we are still the victims. I hope that someone finds a little peace in reading this book and can release some of the anger that's inside. There are too many children hurting in this world from abuse maybe they can understand the cry that's heard over the land of so much abuse and do something. Probation will not stop the molesting of our babies court ordered monitoring of offenders will help this age old problem of sexual abuse the hidden crime am writing this book not because what has happen to me but because of all the injustice I see every day. I never told of my abuse until now I was afraid and just let it go but there are so many who can't let go and it rips their lives apart. There are difference kinds of abuse but no form is justified anyone knowing of someone who has been abused are being abused please report it.

We must examine are selves and see what we can do to help the fight against abuse compassion we have but involvement we need. Stop, Look, and Listen for any child being abused and do something about it. Knowing as you read this book someone child is being abused continue to push until it gets the proper attention it needs. I read a passage that said evil is all about and it was right there are scentless acts of abuse every day all over the world. Wanting to help is only human doing something about it is only right until we get justice it's alright to tell. Break the silence come out of hiding contact any law enforcement center if you think any kind of abuse might be happening. Bring wrong is far better than being right and not doing something about it. When someone loses hope they are divested and when there is no hope there comes destruction. Where do the victims go for their probation what relief do they have. This is an outrageous are justice system needs to look at the massage their sending the predators. More has to be done to stop the cruel punishment to the victims. Who is there to hold them when they can't sleep? Turning to any means possible to stop the pain. I ask the question if it was their child what Would they do. Let's secure the future of our children and stop them from falling through the cracks of the justice system. With all the stories and cases none of it makes any difference if laws are not changed. Are the answers we are getting significant enough? The mission is to increase the level of attention and voices are support for all children worldwide they need are help. It's a battle but we can conquer it and win lets be heroes in are own communities with no hesitation stopping the injustice of abuse. Protection that's the word we are looking far who is protecting our children? What kind of protection and from whom? The fight must continually go on until something happens. This is a crucial time and should be treated as such the scares left on an abused child nothing is acceptable are significant enough to we get justice.

WHERE DO WE GO FROM HERE

Where do we go engaging and empowering the community is the goal be a part of service heighten awareness and get involved. The time is crucial increased awareness the problem will decrease marching and protesting against child abuse, child pornography, child labor. Let's stop the crying of the children by any means it's time far a change when we remain silent there will be no change. Better education on sexual abuse stricter laws, programs set up therapy and treatment centers, I haven't heard of them yet. The more attention focused on the problem the less you have it's about time someone recognizes the children tomorrow is too late. Where are the activists against child abuse when our babies are still crying? Offenders are still walking the streets. More and more victims are coming fourth and far them to have the courage to come justice should prevail. I read that said when the courts become a mockery and the guilty are set free it's the duty of our citizens to step in. While officials ponder over issues statewide task forces should be preparing ways to reduce the numbers of cases. But until this happens the cry will still be heard over the land of hurting and abused children stop it's more than enough. Our children are becoming more and more invisible every day in a fight to find and answer where do we start. Just look at all the cover up its noticeable and can't not be missed how do we comprehend this refusing to stop and not take no for an answer. Missing and exploited children enough we must no longer take probation for an answer we must give accountability for ourselves. Abuse leaves bitterness and lost of directions the storms in a Childs life after abuse is critical we must find the strength to endure. We are not defeated with the right guidance all the dissatisfaction of all the cases that don't get justice we still can win. No more Jane doe so lets put abuse on display keep molesters in the spot light we can't win the battle unless we have the courage to stand and fight the war. Not only children there are so many adults with the pain of abuse still ripping their lives apart .The drive I have inside of me keeps me wanting to do whatever I can to help stop all the injustice. I have family members who been raped victims friends, and what about the ones we have not heard about. Communities have to unite raise awareness stop the violation of our babies' bodies the damage is more serious the self esteem, guilt, and unworthiness than anyone could imagine. My low self esteem triggered a lot of things in my life that should have been different. I was terrified most of my life not knowing were this road would lead me when will I get my justice?

AWARENESS

Staying committed and not getting frustrated or exhausted are the traumatic effects of abuse. We need to recognize early signs and get the support needed for victims when confronted with all the stopping blocks. We need definite answers and to maintain are goal which is getting the legislation and prosecution to recognize the disturbing numbers and come up with recommendations that can be put in effect. We can triumph over abuse by monitoring the offenders the struggle can be over by stopping so many predators from walking the streets. This is a critical time and we must act now so much abuse has gone unpunished and probated pushed aside as if it wasn't a major concern. Better foundations and proposals can increase awareness and with all the disturbing factors we all need to confront and take responsibility. The devastation of abuse is enough by itself to make someone do something about it. The best prevention is to focus on the predator and maintain a close watch and it will make a difference. Child molestation endangers the emotional and physical health of a child. We can reduce the numbers if we focus on the cause of the abuse if we can stop the abuser then the healing can begin. We have the printed out facts about child abuse medical resource centers but how does this help a child that has just had their body ripped apart. What part does this play? How do they soften the pain? There are offenders probated on the streets they are not being watched are monitored how does the impact of this soften the pain? There are psychological and behavioral problems of this crime answer we need more attention focused abuser more media coverage and newspaper articles could expose these predators. Lets focus more on the humiliation the victims has to suffer during and after they have been molested it's very painful. Embarrass the predator and put them to shame and watch them and see if it makes a difference of how fast they molest again. The impact might have a bigger effect than we think no more pat on the hand. Who will be responsible for letting these predators walk the streets?

The time is now the children can't wait any longer the mission should be a vision for the children future finding a better approach by addressing the undenying fact that too many children are being abused. Members of congress, the Supreme Court, and the legislature are legally and morally responsible for the abuse that plagues this country. The prosecutors shouldn't settle for probation without monitoring it should be a law. They need to enforce any means possible to insure and prevent the consistency of abuse which is growing rapidly every day We must demand our government and legislation to take responsibility and be accountable for the abuse that our children have to suffer. We can successfully wage war sexual abuse despite the negative numbers. These are critical times when the courts and prosecutors are stumbling over whether to incarcerate or probate. Our community should be working harder and encouraging each other that whatever they can do is significant enough. Just coming fourth and reporting whatever you might know we will win the fight over abuse. There is so much damage being done just come anything will and can make a difference. We must emphasize the the importance of treatment centers if more attention isn't focused on abuse it will spread through this country like a plague lets put a stop to this problem now. I am definitely getting stronger from the things that I have experienced and the abused children and adults I have come in contact with. But to live it and be around it is more devastating than you could imagine there should be ongoing investigations in every case the massage is increasingly clear. Offenders need to be in treatment this enables survivors to better rebuild their lives. The emotional effects alone would be more beneficial in the recovery of the victims.

PREVENTIONS AND TREATMENTS

Increased public awareness and improved resources rape, molestation. And sodomy are all in violation of ones rights and are against the law. Sometimes it's so overwhelming it can take over your very being. The public must become involved to help insure the future of our children. Something has haywire in a nation that seems to have forgot about our children and the suffering they are enduring. We must sacrifice and stop our children from being miserable and made a mockery of and the invasion of their bodies. Maybe we can make tremendous progress by submitting proposals to our government and congress. How long will a nation be arrogant to the pain and agony that is plaguing our nation's children? Immediate action is necessary to protect the integrity of a country of crying and waiting children. We must confine, extinguish, and rescue our children from sexual abuse. Congress has a right to pass nay bill or amendment and there is a lot of work to be done and the mission must not be taken lightly. Sexual abuse is climbing at a rate that is unbelievably high and the victims and are communities to better protected. There has to be a better way of establishing ideas on how to confine and treat sex offenders. Our children are worthy under the United States constitution to be protected.

Immediate action is needed to preserve and give back their dignity and stops the pain of those who are trying to fight back. Protecting them from the judicial system that probates their offenders my hope is someone will find strength in knowing that it's is alright to tell. The subject is very delicate but we must continually pursue the cause, and be effective we have to maintain the courage to stomp out abuse of any kind. The justice systems are felling tragically which is very disturbing should we discredit the government for not focusing enough on our country being plagued by sexual offenders. This is jeopardizing the health, life and wellbeing of our children the damage is hard to repair and in some cases it can't be repaired.Raped, molested, incest, although my body has healed my mind never will forget. Everything that happen to me I kept inside and denied ever happen to me trying to run and hide but it never goes's away. There are so many that suffer from abuse the staggering numbers should be enough to demand immediate on going investigations. I am writing this book on child sexual abuse hoping maybe it will help abused victims come fourth and any child that is being abused. And that they don't have to be afraid it's time to stop letting offenders walk away untounched.We are fighting to stop abuse but in the struggle we need to be marching against probation without monitoring. And before we start finding more of our babies bodies ripped apart then who will take the blame. We live in a time where everything is so open that nothing should be hidden away in secret any more.Sex is open youe sexual preference is open far display so sexual abuse should be open and displayed to help stop offenders from molesting our children. But until we find a way to stop it the cry of are babies will be heard over the land of hurting and abused children STOP IT'S MORE THAN ENOUGH.

CONSISTENCY

Consistency is the only way we can stomp out child sexual abuse the fight must continue until justice prevails. Offenders should be treated for this disease as soon as possible left untreated it will spread. There is no explanation on why there isn't on going treatment and monitoring of all offenders. But the welfare of our children is at stake and the importance of treatment centers must be emphasized and we must let this be known. When you have been a victim and have talked to others you have a understanding of all the bitter feelings and pain. It's a disgrace to see how family is abusing family brothers, abusing sisters, fathers sexual abusing their own children and it goes on. You don't have to look far to see abuse It's hard to cope sometimes but knowing you don't have to do it along will make a big difference. If it wasn't such a big cover up it would be easer to deal with and maybe more cases would be reported.

But both girls and boys face many problems confused about their identity and what there place in life will be. Can you even imagine the pain and embarrassment? Woman struggle but what about the babies and young men the devastation and rage they have to indure just to keep on going. I talked with a young man and saw the pain and bitterness he tried to hide from me he told me what had happen to him as a young man over and over again by his own family. This has made him very confused and angry and he is very sexually active trying to prove and maintain his man hood. It's very hard for him to cope he lost his identity as a young boy and doing anything to get it back. The experience takes over body and mind the shame makes it harder to report it. This happen to him when he was a young boy now this man craves sex just to prove his manhood. But what kind of man will he become who can he hold accountable for what has happen to him.

The cry and devastation, rage confusion, struggle for identity it's a very dangerous problem to deal with. Never realized that I had lost my identity until later on in my life. I just put everything inside and blocked it out as if it never happen never talked about it until a lot of years have passed put it in the back of my mind hoping no one would find out. There is a disturbing epidemic of abuse in this country and there isn't enough being done to stop it. How can we make a change? Neglet, Mistreatment of our children must stop now. Fighting for a cure to free our children from abuse, Restricting offenders from living are working in a distance of the victim this will not stop the crime until predators are the main focus. They will still molest we have all the websites we have registered offenders yet the abuse goes on. The sad news most of the predators are set free and justice has no regret and the molestation goes on.

How can finding a cure for abuse be possible when the offenders are free? Justice sure does prevail for the predators. End abuse children suffer in silence how many do you know? Do we have to negotiate with the justice system to make them more committed? Having offenders put in treatment we must not stop until it happens determined that every case be examined and decide how the treatment will apply. All options must be examined before the release of an offender. It's the ultimate responsibility of our legislation and congress to set in motion with significant accountability to be responsible for prevention centers to treat and monitor these offenders.

Global organization striving to free our children from abuse determined to see the numbers drop with information on how many are being abused and the effects it has on them. But who has the answers to stop the offenders? Will they provide information on how and when the pain will stop the biggest percentage do victims have no answers that will make a difference. The ones I came in contact with no one had reported anything so if you are to afraid to tell and ashamed if someone abuses you. What happens to the ones that tried to take their own lives and said they didn't want to live anymore? Can the information that is supplied help? What about the 2 year old that has been brought in the emergency room broken bones sexually abused whets going to happen to their offender? Abuse it's hard to recognize finding help shouldn't be.

Sexual abuse should be nationally recognized state and local laws are established to protect this is their obligation to see that our communities are protected by any means possible. Rehabilitation programs and centers that mandatory demand sexual offender to attend road to recovery programs and their victims. Without treatment there is no recovery some of the victims strive to find help for such horrible acts of abuse some unbearable to speak of. No child should have to be hurting from abuse. Speak up voice your concern wake up the government the administration makes them take a good look at what is happening. Should the distress signal be put in effect it's very necessary monitoring is the best recommendation and keeping all citizens aware. Most undetected crime of all because most victims will not tell what's happening to them. Every child and adult wants to know how to get pass what has happened and move on. We need amber alerts when some ones child has been abused justice we need it to make sure predators go into treatment.Justic to place the pictures of the offenders on billboards and television, justice to make sure these offenders don't go unpunished, justice for hope knowing that there is hope without logging onto the internat.If someone calls for help all areas of help should be available whenever needed. Sweet justice where were you when my baby was molested and no one was ever punished foe that crime? Sweet justice she still cries sometime where are you? She still jumps when I come in her bedroom where are you I can't find you? Shouldn't have to be this way can she be assured that her offender will be put in jail and treated for this crime? Are will she have to pass him on her way to recovery justice where are you hope that justice will hear her cry and work harder to insure our babies that every effort has been put in place to make sure that their pain will not go unpunished. It's there looking us right in the face. I have worked around sex offenders they are very sick minded people .Abused, raped, molested it's not a good felling everything seems so hopeless and you try to figure out which way to turn. Wondering if this is the end are can you find the beginning of healing and living a normal life again.

The mission is to provide ways of preventing child abuse making offenders aware of the consequences of committing these crimes. So I ask with classes in the prison systems how this will make a difference without ongoing treatment and monitoring this will insure the safety of our babies? Not enough programs resources and time spent on abuse there are so many plans but not and effective course of action. Read all the facts go over this n umbers but better public awareness and better laws will help the prevention of abuse. Offenders on the front page and watch how they relate to having there faces and names on front page news. We need citizens in every community to band together and fight Their has to be a turning point somewhere. There should be less website information and more hands on and more news reports give the offenders their glory front page headlines. We can be hard speak up speak loud enough and you will be heard save a child from this crisis while our babies continue to sink deeper and deeper into the cracks of the justice system their bodies and mind lost. The research and experts so called if you haven't been there you can't be an expert. We need you on Capitol Hill fighting to get a bill passed that focuses more on the predators of our children. Advocates fighting more for felons being released without ongoing treatment programs because of system full felons and no treatments. What does this tell us about are law makers and justice? Ongoing monitoring facilities are an essential part of knowing something is being done that will make a difference. Abuse is so wide spread and getter everyday look into your on family and you might be very surprised at what you might find. Confused and struggling to separate what is right and wrong trying to move on but in what direction and what effect will this have on our children.

The episodes of abuse are outrageous and we must come forward amend help stomp out abuse with any means possible it is extremely urgent. It's unacceptable the numbers of cases that go unreported scream, yell, whatever it takes let it be known that you have been violated and that you demand justice it's your right. Organizations need more input and reach out more in the community and let victims know that someone is there and cares. Open your hearts our babies need freedom from being tortured and their little bodies ripped apart but yet it's still happening everyday. How do we give them hope and stop the hurt th3e burden is so hard to carry lets give them something to hold on to. Our lives begin to end the day we become silent about the things that matter being aware of what's happening around us and doing something about it. That's the hope that our children need. Change starts when someone has the courage to stand up and say no and putting the offenders in treatment and appealing to the legislature and encourage each other not to stop. Until we make a difference and that we do have a voice and will be heard. We need offenders in rehab widely publicized keeping the public aware of whom these predators are will make a head start in protecting their family. Most citizens rarely know what these offenders even look like who are they protecting. Until we all get outraged and very disgusted about what is happening to our children and make something change abuse will still plague are country. Help from are government, legislature, and judicial system to stop abuse for all are children and anyone who has been abuse. As I ask before justice stand up we want to see you, where are you? Trying to find a profile of my predator on TV the newspaper, can't find one just heard pieces of what happen. Justice stand up so I can see you it still hurts and when I finally come back out to try to go on thought I saw my predator smiling at me. Take hold of me justice I need you were are you to catch me when I fall. When I was crying in my bed last night I thought about you, there should be better sources to broadcast offenders of sexual abuse. I meet a sexual offender in the hospital that was trying to expose his self to me is he just getting back from treatment are had he never been? It was once said as there's another days living there's still time to do something and make a difference. We must stand up for what we believe in even if we stand along keep pushing to end abuse in any form.

Why is it so hard to comprehend when will society recognize and be aware of the pain our children are endurning. Justice where are you when will you do something and stop our babies from being molested every day? Can you tell me what's next did you see the pictures that was broadcasted last night? I must of missed it. Recovery is to see are offenders pay in treatment, and monitored to see that they don't molest our children again. There are so many children being molested now it's hard to keep up with them get in somebodies business and help stop the pain but first we must stop the problem. We live in a puzzling world no child should have to fight for their virginity and have their little bodies torn apart and not even know what is happening to them. Who will put their pieces back together and make the whole again will their body parts ever fit right again. Neglect is a form of abuse in that notes this country is guilty of neglecting our babies. A child is being abused as you read this book more media coverage wake up we need are nation to focus on what's important. Nothing is more news worthy than the health and well-being of our children. What better service can we offer them? There is a force behind our babies and that is are citizens and are selves. It's all right to tell and have the community stand up and fight with you. What about the 3 year old that was molested by her fathers friend news flash never heard about it again I talked with the father he ask me why I had no answer justice where are you? What justice will this baby have she can't speak up and name her offender are identify him who will. Someone has to stand up and fight foe the ones that can't. We must take the upper hand and see that babies like this one will have justice. How do you recover from your babies being abused and their little bodies violated and ripped apart. When does it get better when predators are being monitored not just jailed and set free to molest again with no remorse. Recovery starts when justice prevails until these changes are made things will not change.

Hope that offenders will be put on front page and not hidden away Americas most wanted sex offenders and molesters off the streets. Child services investigating any report of abuse and being involved as long as it takes and not let these children fall back in the hands of their offenders.

So many children have been put back and have been horribly abused and some lost their lives. Hope that someone will read this book and it will make a difference. Hope that lives will be changed and our children will be protected and justice will prevail foe all and our children will stop hurting from abuse. Hope the justice system realize that when predators pay for their crimes and sitting in a treatment center just maybe they will think before committing such horrible act of abuse again. We have a war in Iran against our solders and we have a war in this country against our children fighting for their virginity and to be free from abuse. Too many of are children are falling through the cracks in the justice system if they only new how much they were hurting maybe more attention would be focused on this every growing problem. Knowledge to protect their privacy but not to cover it up we most have a sense of ownership and share the responsibility of helping maintain a safe environment for our children. Supporting and recognizing and providing the best means of understanding possible.

RECOVERY WHEN

Our strongest defense against abuse is watching out for what is happening around us and making sure we do something about it. Without any hesitation getting the message out that our children are slipping away. We have an instant to protect our children but when we fail who will be there to take are place. Abuse is with us every day and staring us in the face but will we recognize it and the decades of abuse that have been hidden away. Reality has come to life the time is now to end the struggle of innocent children trying to escape and heal. It's unbelievable the struggle and suffering from the hands of a predator and mostly in their own family. This is personal to me coping with what has happen to me and seeing what this is doing to so many children in this country. Uncover abuse and it's predators set a nation of abused children free it takes love, courage, and strength to overcome this disgusting act of abuse. Where is the outrage? In this nation abuse is out of control statistics show how many are estimated to be abused but does it tell you how much it will hurt. The breaking point is here no more senseless acts of abuse it shouldn't be tolerated any more. Better awareness preventing the fatalities of molesting and founding our baby's laws that will stand up for them and see that they get justice.

Can you hear their cry it's loud enough to hear across the nation hope that extreme measures will be take to stop their cry. Speak up a logo in the children hospital read they need are voices to set them free. Voices over America we can speak foe them have the courage to step forward and change a Childs life. It's a challenge we must face and conquer the courage to stand up and say no more to the slow response of are congress and lesglature. Committed to not letting child abuse be back page to the media and to coverage committed to making sure neighborhoods are safe for our children. How much longer must our children stay in limbo waiting for a change while the abuse is ripping their bodies apart? We should have rage over the fact that the communication isn't faster and more affective not knowing and recognizing the urgent need to act. This puts victims at a higher risk of being violated I have rage inside of me with what I see and remembering what has happen to me. In a world of confusion and dismay if we all just could leaned a hand and get in some bodies business and save a child. What about the ten year old that I talked to that was raped and simonized but refused to tell by who because it had happen before so it didn't matter and no one cares. The three year old that was raped and beat to death by her fathers friend. The young man I talked to every day who was repeatedly raped by family members now questions his own man hood. The young girl who was molested most of her life and became a prostitute and drugs.

The young woman who says she no longer wants to live because life is to hard to cope with the lady who I know that has to face her offender that just lives down the street from her wondering why she has to feel guilty having done nothing wrong. What about the little babies that has had their little bodies ripped apart and wondering why it hurts so badly who will stand accountable foe them. All most every day I come face to face with abuse where the experts and justice are. That will enforce a strong and powerful bill that will make every predator stop and think. Social workers getting more involved in their cases and stop letting so many children die from the hands of their predator. Attention our babies are being molested everyday there has to be and end soon.

HIDDEN SCARES

Hidden scares that no one will never know about so many different cultures a hidden epidemic it's overwhelming and should be stop. So many of us have broken spirits who can justify the victimization of our babies. The time is now there's not enough information being shared in are communities from officials and the government. The high expectation we have from are government failing badly community involvement will be are tower of strength to step forward and make a difference. To accomplish the gold we set out to do we need more attention focused on the hidden secrets. A few years back sexual abuse was the big family secret that shouldn't be told this is the 20th century everything is up front even your sexual preferance.Sexual abuse is every bodies business lets stop the hidden terror press on and have the courage to fight and win. The upmost importance of urgency is needed to insure the focus will not end. The unidentified must be identified and justice must win over evil far to long victims have been overlooked we view ourselves as broken but yet we are still hold. Endurance is the factor of not being overlooked and filed away innocent but struggling to free ourselves from the situation are body and mind have been subject to.

Then we are experts the experts in everything was once a beginner you can't tell me how bad that it hurt when I was raped and better unless you have been there. Devastating yes you feel it zero tolerance is absolutely essential and abuse should no longer be overlooked can you hear their cry? The full support of our legislature to insure a bill that can be endorsed to passionately recognize the urgency of putting a stop to abuse of all kinds that is infecting our country. There is a lack of judgment, compassion and understanding a skeptical nation on sexual matters has got to turn critical the mission is to positively impact the health and well-being of a nation pledged by abuse. Give a child the change foe a happy and normal life by ridding this country of predators that pray on our babies. The anguish they feel overlooked by are experts and government were they in my room last night did they watch me shake in my bed afraid someone might come in my room? Were the experts there to give me a shoulder to cry on are something to make it better. The experts that knows how it feels to have your little body ripped apart and no one seems to care. Were Our you experts hold up your head overlooked when the predator that molested you walks the same streets that you do and you could meet them anytime. They have no remorse for what has happen to you and would molest again if the chance came along. Overlooked all the traumatized children that can't get a grip on life the crisis is getting worse and still being pushed aside as as if is unimportant very frustrating. Still the numbers are rising are justice system keeps down playing abuse probating to many operators.

Nationwide alerts on are justice system beaten, raped, molested and left behind where is justice? You need to stand up where are you hiding? Walk on justice why are the numbers rising look in are courts and behind the bench and filter out what you find. Overlooked the facts more lawmaker's laws. Someone should walk in my shoes one day the people I meet and the stories they tell you would not believe. I am an expert raped yes more than once I have been with children, woman, and even men that have been molested justice you should have been there to play Your part. Hidden away in our minds but our children are still racked with pain waiting to tell but afraid because of the world we live in. Inspire hope for our children and be aware of your surroundings and most of important get involved. Stop the cover up of the facts break the cycle raise awareness to the highest point the threat level is very high are babies needs to be saved from the justice system. Raise the red flag break the silence uncover the truth about the offenders and not let them hide anymore. Fight until we find justice where are you? Who gives you the right to let my offender walk the street? And judge what has happen to me and how it felt do you know how it feels to sit beside the father, grandfather, brother our neighbor who has been molesting you. Knowing how it is eating at your body and soul feeling like your insides are coming out. Let me shout and tell my story tell some names and try to get my justice where were you when I was raped by my mothers boyfriend. Molested and fondled by one of my grandparents and trying to stay out of reach of the rest of the family. If I would of told at that time would I have gotten my justice? We need time to mend are wounds meet our offenders on the streets. Where is the aggressiveness of citizens and parents that just want take anymore and stop standing by letting our babies be mangled and abused ignoring all the facts and signs.

Yes it's alright to tell let them feel some of the shame and embarrassment that you face everyday. Global warning sexual abuse is at an all time high more awareness is crucial to the pain. Ask how many were molested last night that no one is aware of, how many didn't tell because they sure afraid to come fourth. How many said if they did tell would it make any difference. How many were too young to tell and living a life of tournament needing someone to intervene on their behalf and stop the pain. How much longer must a nation of child abuse goes on when will are government come together hand in hand with citizens and then we can make a difference. Put a face on abuse for the entire world to see and it will make a difference. Still waiting to be free from the bondage of abuse and the justice system shall we walk with our children's pictures around are necks with signs of molested and left behind waiting on justice.

Waiting on another child to be abused and not cone forward waiting for laws to change that will give us a peace of mind knowing that all is done that can be do. Knowing that we have a government that will stand behind us no matter what tired of hearing of our babies being molested and killed. Waiting on a nation of children to stand up and say no more and names their offender and not be afraid are ashamed anymore and feel good about it knowing that it is alright to tell. Who will apologize for all the pain and suffering of the children? Who can say sorry for not taking enough time to listen and see the discuss and pain we are going through. Apologize how many lives have been lost? How many children will committee suicide before someone steps in and takes another look. This disease is spreading through are country so rapid and not controlled. Who will apologize for all the lives that have been lost? It's hard to comprehend the massacre of our children's bodies there has to be no tolerance when it comes to the safety and well being of our children. Our judicial system is a step behind the abuse that is ragging through are country like wild fire who will we hold accountable. The tragedy is no one really listens to what is happening everyday around us the government should be criticized for falling short of protecting and making sure that they stay in the head lines would make a big difference.

This global crisis demands accountability leadership that we can depend on and take on abuse and history it and its source. Why in a world so advance child abuse runs so rapid our babies can be man handled and their tiny body parts ripped apart. It's a collision course they are on and time is very crucial we need serious commitment their lives are being put in jeopardy every day. Despite the economic crisis are nation still stands strong we have the ability and adversity to end abuse.

Every child matters and maybe someday they can be free from abuse and have a promising future. The sexual abuse in this country is very unreal and can strike at any moment taking another body are life. Listen can you hear it the cry the pain and frustration it carries with it. We have to get the right massage out that there are some fighting to stop the pain and give them hope. I know the rage of wondering what to do and which way to turn the humiliation is enough to take over your body and mind. Breaking the cycle of abuse letting the world know that we will not hide away anymore the only way to fight abuse is to face it head on. Put and alert on the predator monitor them and let everyone know who they are and what has happen. Uncover the silent cry of our children and let it be known they have been victimized and want their justice. Tragically thousands of die every year of abuse sad and shocking but true we demand are congress to face this problem and break down the percentage of abused children. Where is the outrage over the senseless deaths and molestation of our babies? Sadly we don't have to look far to find abuse break down the cases and lets save one child at a time. To protect our children is to safe guard the future of our country there is a war on land and children. Do we need congress to send in the troops if necessary to stop the killing and slaughter of our babies? Just look around and see all the fatalities identify, persecute, and lock up safe guard our children together we can make it happen.

An article read about the number of soldiers killed in Iran the numbers are very high and so much concern. But where is the outrage over the number of our youngest citizens being molested and slaughtered right here on are home land. Poverty hunger and so much more it's a fight just to stay alive do they have to fight for their virginity to enough is not the word it's more than enough. Can you even imagine they pain and the cry it's loud enough if you visited a hospital and watched as they come in, if your child had just been raped and was still shaking would you listen? Stop the war on our children they fight every day to be tree from their abuser maybe troops need to be deployed across the nation to protect our most prized procession our children. We cannot let this cycle of abuse continue there is no secret anymore nothing to be ashamed of sexual abuse is a crime and should be treated as such. Our current generation is so much more out spoken about sex and anything else coming fourth shouldn't be as hard to do.

The number of deaths in child abuse with the number of deaths in Iran our children are slipping away who will be left to fight a war. More focus on the children's behalf are president making sure there's enough funding among are country so there will be know child left behind every child matters . Children should all ways have a choice and futures let's make sure we all do are parts and make it happen. If the focus was more on the molestation of our babies instead of who was in the news and won the game last night are who cheated just maybe we could save a child from abuse. As long as we have the feeling of worthlessness are predators have the means of controlling are lives embrace every concept of life keep your guard up and speck for what you believe in and not be intimidated anymore for those who can. In search to find a cure for all diseases we face child abuse which should be among the stop. This is a hard core world and our babies are being eaten alive as a mother. Father someone has to stand up and say enough and mean it. There are so many more headed for destruction we need to stand against all obstacles and never give up. It's an obligation we all must bear do we need better government that will fight and be more committed to winning.

Giving our children hope and a chance for a rewarding life there has to be an escape route that leads to their freedom. Complete commitments the innocents of our babies are at hand without a dough abuse is ragging across are land. We have all the wed sites what's the use we need aids and for it to be publicized get the message out for all to see. Only we can stop abuse better awareness, reporting anything and anybody where things just don't seem right. I had rather be wrong and report it than to be right and not and let an innocent child be molested. Together we can change the world of abuse just open are eyes and hearts our children are endangered species from their own kind. Predators stalking their pray ready to attack at any time their lives are being threaten as if they were animals in the wild. Losing their indemnity to a world that is pledged by child abuse. The twisted minds and behavior of sexual predators what quality of life will our children have. Pressure and time must be put on are legislature better effects to stop this disaster that is happening to our future the children. The victory can be won the impact that we have are voices can change the world the battle is not lost although the war is still ragging and it is a heavy load to carry. We can defeat it before it poses a bigger threat to our babies wake up America child abuse is taking over this country while we stand idle by and watch it happen. Stop it's enough more than a enough and it's alright to tell.

COMMITTED

Committed to stopping the trauma that our children have to endure making a difference stop watching baby after baby being brought in the emergency and not doing anything about it. It should be personal to everyone how does it make you feel when a three year old babies body has been ripped apart. Committed to making sure sticker penalties are put in place that will make a predator stop and think. Making sure victims have every access to whatever help they need and not feeling ashamed about it. Helping services go on and not look back and make a new start knowing that they have someone standing behind them to help. Despite the challenge they still have to face another day. Together we can protect Gods most precious gift our babies. Persistence and a will to stop them from suffering any longer there is a child being molested every second. Please take a stand in a world so hateful and cruel report it one at a time. That's one less that will have to suffer from the hands of an offender. Uncovered and not hidden away anymore suffer not the little children If I could I would my loving arms around you and keep you safe.

Life is a terminal illness and we all are waiting to exit this world. Please lets help stomp out abuse and any acts of violence that we can. Fragile handle with care damaged goods need repair should this be stamped on are children and a transcript sent to are law makers and congress. The devastation of what is happening should be enough to make a nation stop and wonder what is going on with our children and why it is taken so lightly. Blame it is like a national disaster who is guilty ourselves, government, our experts the legislature needs to step forward and takes it's place passing a bill that is acceptable and strong and will change the course of abuse. Should we blame sociality for keeping abuse covered up not treated like any other crime? The lives of so many children are lost and left behind to suffer the consequences living on the edge looking for a way out. Who do we blame? The most over looked crime and war on our children what kind of world do we live in we need congress to stick their noses in and fight for our children. Abuses we need to take are places and the time is now stop watching so many of our babies still being tormented how can are government sleep at night. Investigation, prosecution, someone has to run interception for them are president said that the war in Iran was almost over but when will the war on our children end. There was a passage that I read on a bill of sexual rights we have to what happens to are body, a right to say yes are no and have control of what happens to you.

What happens when it gets ripped away from you? And you have to fight for better laws. All the books that have been published on child abuse were are we now there is so much abuse still tarring apart lives it's devastating. Global awareness why is there so little attention on child abuse? Wake up we need a crackdown on child abuse and make every case top priority the cover will end and maybe our babies will be safe. Committed to making every child feels safe and knowing that it is alright to tell and if they are violated please come fourth and tell. This is my story very aggravated and appalled to what is still happening in mind I blame myself for all that has happen to me the rapes and molestation of my body. Today I think of it but go on but will never forget the trials I went through if I had known it was alright to tell I would have saved myself a lot of pain and grief. My mother deserved to know what was happening to me that's why I feel so guilty and ashamed it's all right to tell and set your mind free.

The best help there is to talk about it and gets those bustards of the streets and get convicted, Incent, molested, rape they all come under the same headlines abuse. I talk about how to cope but what about the babies who will come fourth for them. What quality of life will they lead and what will their minds be like who will be there to catch them if they fall. E must not sit by any longer and watch what is happening and not do are parts and save a child from being abused and hidden away. A black white girl boys it really doesn't matter their bodies are still being explored and abused it's not prejudice and passes through the rich and poor. Taking over our baby's virginity and leaving so much destruction in its path. We have been for warned this is happening and it shell strike again so we must be prepared and stop it from distorting so many lives. Time is critical every parent, government official, needs to stop and realize just how critical abuse is can you hear how loud their crying?

No one hears my cry
No one hears as the days go by
When the door opens I know what's in store
I don't think I can take any more
Who can I turn to who can I trust
The pain goes on from morning to dust

Devastating the effects of abuse with children and the elderly we must understand what is happening to them. They are very vulnerable and their cry for must be heard we can control the cry by controlling the predator. The mission is to stop abuse in its tracks and not tolerate it anymore. The Megan Law is good but our babies are still being molested and falling short of being protected. Profiling the offender Bill Boarding, and monitoring laws that will make a offender stop and take another look. Mothers stand up and take your places stop letting these bastards get away with the slaughter and molestation of your babies .It starts from you those are your babies justice has nothing to do with that. Better justice well less fight for it all the way to capital hill makes some noise and gets some bills passed. What do you think that does to a little childs body can't you feel it makes your skin crawl are you on your way? If we as mothers stand up and take our places and take control of what's happening to our children. The justice system want hold your babies the government can't hear them when they cry and can't sleep at night. It is up to the mothers of this country to put a stop to the molestation of their children. We have more of a voice than we think it's time to use it talk about making a difference walk on mothers and free your babies. We are the ones that they expect to be there to protect them catch them and make everything right. The government is falling short but as parents we must get out there and be noticed and make a difference. The laws that are there to protect us will prevail and do their jobs there is still too many waiting to be heard. There are still a lot of mothers who are lost victims themselves and still trying to find their way but for those of us who still stand tall we can make a difference. Believe that the rage inside of us will fight for the children and their offenders will stop walking the same streets as they do to molest and kill again with no remorse.

Free us from the rage we feel
Please free us before they kill
Free us from the pain inside
Please free us before they hide

Author

Notify

Notify but will it help

Laws that let you know that sex offenders live in your community yes we have a right to know that our child could be molested at any given time. Maintain a close watch on your childs neighborhood they need regular monitoring why should predators' have more rights to living a life uninterrupted? And free of all when our babies still struggle yet to sleep at night. Who give the legislation the right to protect offenders trying to make their lives better while we struggle not to kill those bastards? What special rights and gratification are they allowed to have? The only rights a convicted sex offender should have is to report and be monitored and have their actives tracked. Convicted sex offender if given the chance will molest again ripping our children's bodies and lives apart. This is when legislation needs to place limitations on the whereabouts of these predators how many rights do they really have? All the books on registering and notification of offenders are there but the molestation of our babies goes on. Who will be held accountable for that? This is not like a witch hunt to hunt down and burn at the stake but maybe it should be treated like one.

I know the pain of watching our justice that lets the bastard who molested my child walk the streets with no morels about what has happen. Hopefully this book will have a strong impact on all victims to not let these molesters hide anymore and let it be known who they are. And maybe congress and the legislation will finally see all the work that still has to be done to stop their bodies from being ripped apart. Increasing intervention maximizing the resources to improve the outcome and quality of life for our children. This epidemic has very serious side effects we don't hear it every day but it's still ragging. In the beginning of the nineteen century there was a summit held on the health and welfare of our children at the rate of the climbing numbers of abuse and neglect it's time for another one. President, legislation, and congress stop turning your heads nationally the media would have a tremendous impact across the nation on uncovering offender's crimes against our children. Communities should notify of offenders for the purpose of watching out and protecting their children. Talk about the offenders rights what rights to live a normal and happy life in our neighborhoods. While their victims can't sleep at night remembering what has happen. Talk about rights who's rights? They have a right to no vigilantism but we have to know Notification laws only notify you of their presence it will not stop the molesting of our babies. Notify me when you can tell me that those bastards are being mortared of their whereabouts.

Sexual pray for a child will not change if you lock them up it's an addition you can't stop. If a wild animal pray is blood putting them in a cage want stop the animal from wanting blood. Child molesters prey on children and just because we lock them up want stop the taste of wanting a child. Notify me when you can tell me what purpose they play in the society we live in. Wondering when they will strike again can you tell me that? Notify me when there are noi more secrets, child molestation has to stop and the time is now and crucial to our children. For the safety and welfare of our children we have the right to know.

> Notify me when repeat offenders move in they will molest again.
> Notify me when the justice system falls to convict they will molest again
> Notify me when predator after predator is being put on probation they will molest again
> Notify me when there's no monitoring of offenders they will molest again.

Child Sexual Abuse

Notify me when another child has been molested and tell me if we have a right to know if sexual predators are being monitored. The focus has to be tough if the numbers are to drop stop trying to protect predators and find a way to keep our children safe. If a thief knows there will be no punishment for stealing they will always steal. We need massive effects to keep our children safe and laws that will enforce them. It has been said that notification violates predator's rights but when they feel free to molest and tear our babies bodies apart who has the rights then? Notification with without monitoring will not keep our children safe.

RIGHTS FOR WHOM

Talk about predator's rights our legislation needs to look back at the record it speaks for its self. They have the right to assault our children and get away with a quick probation. The right to molest again without any hesitations is guilt the right to rob our children of self-respect and the chance to have a normal life. Right to live in your neighborhood while you wonder if your child will be molested from the predator next door. We have the right to know if our constitution is protecting offenders instead of their victims' rights. The right to know that sexual offenders are not put on a pastel and have rights to a normal life. While their victims are still struggling just to sleep at night. When you break the law your rights get suspended the question is do you have any rights after you have torn a little childs body apart. We have a right to have a child protection law put in place that works and that will make a difference. Rights that when we let our children outside knowing that predators are being monitored.

Child sexual abuse can be reduced by keeping your children under a watchful eye knowing where and with who they are with at all times and investigating anyone and anything that might look out of place. Just knowing who's living in your community and knowing that your children have a right to be protected at all times. Rights to know that your neighborhoods are safe and being monitored. Rights to know that we have a congress that will stop letting predators off so easy without any regard to what might happen to your child. You tell me who has the rights? Rights to have justice when you been violated and have to walk by your predator on your way to heal. Our children have a right to be protected and a justice system that will stand behind them and keep them safe.

The anxiety we feel it takes incredible courage to go on and heal but with possible attitudes we can have a normal life and heal. Knowing that we are not along makes a world of difference that there are so many out there just likes you. Help me heal so I can sleep at night help me heal so I can give up the fight. There has to be a compassionate approach to healing their minds and bodies have been through so much emotional trauma. When will congress realize that monitoring sexual offenders is Vidal? To the welfare and healing of our children. Stop the indemnity of our children from being consumed their very being is threaded what kind of humanity will be leading this country? What shape will it be in free their minds and their bodies will heal? How much longer must a nation of sexual abuse go on before are leaders stand up and take another look. Stopping the destructive force that is still targeting our children justice come forward focus more on the ragging numbers of abused children. Understanding the seriousness of sexual abuse and its side effects and the poor response of so many cases will be confronted.

Stop hiding so many offenders behind the so called regal rights, where were my childs legal rights when her body was ripped apart? Child molesters should be convicted not protected give justice where justice is due. Respect confidentiality not cover up BEATEN,BROKEN,RAPED, MOLESTED,AND FORGOTTEN our children are still waiting.

When I was raped by my fathers friend and again by my mothers boyfriend and founded by one of my grandfathers I felt like a vassal that has lost its way not knowing what was happing and why being approached by my own cousin this has a horrible effect on you. Some of it I know was wrong and the rest I just accepted it not knowing what to do afraid to let it be known . How does a 3 are 4 year old child tell something like this when you your self can't understand it. When you grow older then you feel so ashamed and try to keep your secret knowing it was wrong should make it easy but that is far from the truth. I wrote this book poring my heart out trying to let a nation understand how so many children are still hiding. So laws can be put in effect that will make it easy to know that it is all right to tell and something will be done. That we are not the guilty ones and have our predators brought to justice. Stop covering up and protecting our predators and set us free do you ever wonder how many you pass every day that is looking for a way out. Can you see pain in their faces when you have been through it as I have it makes you wonder? How many adults have struggled for so long not to tell but knowing it's the right thing to do.

The cover up trying hot to embarrass your family and just not wanting anyone to know. With doing this we give our predators the right to continue to molest. We all have to come out of the closet as it has been called you are like living a different life than a normal person so much to hold inside. But the time is now in a world of so much not knowing how to end this travesty. Every child deserves to be safe when your child has distress or needs you do anything necessary to help so have the courage to fight for what is right and win. Stop these bastards from molesting our babies stop them from tarring their little bodies apart can you understand that the babies can't speak for themselves. Is this person living beside you while you try to put your baby's body parts back in place? Shell we cover this up? Are his picture on the news and he is being monitoring. Does the community no about this so many different viewpoints on how molesters should be dealt with should they have a say so? Do they have a say so in what rights they have for molesting my child? The resource centers neglect, explored committees' to prevent child abuse our they stopping our children from being stalked? Where are the monitoring devices that keeps offenders in sight at all times or do they have free range to molest at will. What about the safer society how does this apply. What affects our all these prevention agencies having on abuse our children are still crying and no one seems to hear. Yes there are the books but what effects will they have if they don't get in the right hands. What about that child who was raped last night should she get up and go to the library to find help. Will she hear about her molester on a news cast so she will no how to go and get help. We have the child advocacy groups publishing its newsletters but again what effect will it have. The mother who holds her child in her arms after their little body has been torned apart should she looks for a newsletter on abuse. Profiles, news reports, pictures of these molesters and places to go to get help from that's what is needed. Making a difference anyone who wants help will have a better source of help other a web site. Wake up America our babies are hurting lets help them find their way to justice.

VICTIMS

Forget saving the world lets save one child at a time from the millions that are being abused and desperately waiting for help. With welfare and social workers felling short of protecting our children family preservation is just another job. Children are victims of their own society monitoring of molesters would give victims a better defense against safety than just notification. Knowing this may help but will this protect them mortaring will make a dramatic difference and reduce the possibility of another victim. Mandated laws were the offenders' rights will not over shadow the victims. Molester's sick minded psychopath needs treatment as long as it takes maybe a life time to keep our children safe. Victims' have a right to have a molester set up foe whatever treatment they need after the pain and suffering they impose on are babies. Every day is child abuse awareness if you just view some of the images it would make you see why for are victims until we win.

Government has to move more aggressively as the cases come in. exposing these offenders for what they are. There victims who can't remember and just don't want to because of the pain and discuss of it. The young men of sexual abuse abuse hide their pain and cover up the humiliation that consumes their whole being. What kind of father, husband, are citizen will they become without releasing the pain and horror they had to face as

Child Sexual Abuse

a child. What happens when your body reacts to the abuse you know it's wrong but you still have a normal reaction. The destruction of your body and misery that you feel takes away your feeling of self-worth. And you begin to hide within yourself. The rage and anger you feel like the young man who struggles through the pain must come fourth and set their minds and souls free. As victims we must find the strength to stand and take our lives back. Its are right to be heard and free from the humiliation and rage that we fell. The most important thing to remember is that we are the victims here that so many forget. What a battle our babies have to face they can't wait any longer there is no time to be embarrassed, are ashamed. We must stand against our predators and make sure justice prevails. We must stand in defense for our children and stop the molestation and destruction of their bodies they have had more than enough predators, rapist and molesters whatever name head that identifies you will be brought to justice and we will win. Better resources so we can be more able to access the pathway to healing we can take are lives back and go on and have a productive life. We will never forget but we can fight all the obstacles and when we start naming are offenders and making those bastards pay. As a sexual abused child I know what it's wanting someone to stop what is happening to your body. The feeling of being out of place and not feeling worthy of anything just wanting to lust to crawl inside yourself and hide. Wanting to confide in someone but just don't know how and what will be said thinking this only happens to you.

There is an argent need to reach out and respond letting victims know that you will be there. Making sure their voices and justice will prevail knowing they have had more than enough. Children need to cherish the adventure of being a child instead of wondering if someone will still the purity of their bodies. They need something to hang on to motivation is hearing of the success stories and how child abuse is being stomped out. Gives a better feeling knowing something is being done and makes it easier to come fourth. The transition will be challenging but it can be done. Unstoppable that's what we must be our babies are being cheated out of their childhood. Taking on adulthood without knowing what's happening. Someone has to stand in the gap and help reconstruct their fragile bodies. The lack of urgency and poor judgment of child sexual the pain that makes the anger stay inside will never be at peace without justice and the rage will never go away.

> *Raise awareness so the pain will go away*
> *Raise awareness so I can live another day*
> *Raise awareness so I don't have to carry this alone*
> *Raise awareness so I can be safe at home*

I have read the books but the pain and tournament of abuse still goes on so where do we turn now. That's why awareness is so important with are government being aware of all of what has happen and who is responsible there are groups trying to get the rules revised and better inquiries. Advocates urge more investigation and look into the deaths of children and stop the big secret cover-up. Why are so many of our children being abused our children are like the elderly being pushed aside as if their voices don't count and it's not that important enough. Why are there so much denial about what are babies are going through the stories are very painful. And it's very disturbing when so many get away with abusing our babies what is this telling us about are justice system. What about the ones that we haven't heard about justice our children are in immediate danger that will activate the alarm and set them free. What would you do if the unthinkable and unimaginable happen to your child? To fight the war against abuse we must have endurance to stand and not give up with all the discouragement we feel. Obstacles must be pushed down no matter what the cost difficult yes but the time is critical. In a nation that stands powerful and millions of dollars spent on wars and rumors of war. I just know child abuse can be won who will win the prize tonight hopefully our babies will and be set free from abuse of all kinds. Did you hear that ambulance last night? Was it the baby I just heard about its little body broken. Justice Sweet justice where are you? Why is it taking so long?

www.ingramcontent.com/pod-product-compliance
Lightning Source LLC
Chambersburg PA
CBHW052123030426
42335CB00025B/3082